Grace, Fallen from

Wesleyan Poetry

Grace, Fallen from

Marianne Boruch

Wesleyan University Press
Middletown, Connecticut

Published by Wesleyan University Press, Middletown, CT 06459

www.wesleyan.edu/wespress

First Wesleyan paperback 2010

ISBN for the paperback edition: 978-0-8195-6953-0

CIP data appear at the end of the book

Printed in the United States of America 5 4 3 2 1

COVER ILLUSTRATION: Hammershoi, Wilhelm (1864–1916). "Rest," oil on canvas, 1905, 49.5 x 46.5 cm. Photo: Michele Bellot. Photo courtesy of Réunion des Musées Nationaux / Art Resource, NY. Musée d'Orsay, Paris, France.

This project is supported in part by an award from the National Endowment for the Arts

NATIONAL
ENDOWMENT
FOR THE ARTS
A great nation
deserves great art.

—in memory of Don Dunlap, still here

"Only one thing is true: in me, a weight, a little stone."

—Paul Klee

CONTENTS

Grace, Fallen from

A MOMENT

Maybe it's common, this sort
of first meeting. But once, before a guest house
in Germany, the friend
of a friend to come by, and dinner—
that's it, we'll go to dinner, have the famous
spargel, that rare white asparagus, only
in May, our evening pre-arranged by phone,
by email. I need to say again we
hadn't met. Outside I stood
at the door, it being spring, every tree
gloriously poised. And a stranger,
another woman, she too waiting
but near the curb, looking
this way and that, attentive to traffic, hours
from dusk because we were north,
near the sea. And tall, she was towering,
older than I was, hugely
made-up, such meticulous work
behind that elegant finish. Then the friend
of my friend—could that be?—his
parking, his pulling himself
out of that tiny car.
Please understand. I'm usually
right there rushing in, because the world
requires that, loves the quickening
of that. But I was
or I wasn't. Or I was small
but there is smaller. To my left, a door.
Some tree flowering at my right.
I watched as he
to that woman said my name
so charmingly, a question, tilting
his head, *are you . . . ? sorry to disturb,*
are you . . . ? And in that pause—
her vague focusing on him, her loose
finding him now—I leaned forward,

simply curious: what
would she say? smile? yes? tell him yes?
So thread breaks. So water in a glass
clouds and maybe it clears.
So I waited, giving up
everything, to anyone,
just like that.

I

STILL LIFE

Someone arranged them in 1620.
Someone found the rare lemon and paid
a lot and neighbored it next
to the plain pear, the plain
apple of the lost garden, the glass
of wine, set down mid-sip—
don't drink it, someone said, *it's for
the painting.* And the rabbit skull—
whose idea was that? There had been
a pistol but someone was told, no,
put that away, into the box with a key
though the key had been
misplaced now for a year. The artist
wanted light too, for the shadows.
So the table had to be moved. Somewhere
I dreamt the diary entry
on this, reading the impossible
Dutch quite well, thank you, and I can
translate it here, someone writing
*it is spring, after all, and Herr Müller
wants a window of it in the painting,* almost
a line of poetry, I thought even then,
in the dream, impressed
with that "spring after all," that
"window of it" especially, how sweet
and to the point it came over
into English with no effort at all
as I slept through the night. It was heavy,
that table. Two workers were called
from the east meadow to lift
and grunt and carry it
across the room, just those
few yards. Of course one of them
exaggerated the pain in his shoulder.
Not the older, the younger man.
No good reason

to cry out like that. But this
was art. And he did, something
sharp and in the air that
one time. All of them turning then,
however slightly. And there he was,
eyes closed, not much
more than a boy, before
the talk of beauty
started up again.

NEW PAPER

under a pen isn't
snow. I see the real thing
out my window piled up
in cold sunlight. It just isn't.
Isn't a lapse
of anyone's memory though
that might help me sleep. I'm anyone
at night.
                    New paper getting inked up
already with words. Revision: inked up
already with *these* words.
                              But it is, it is
a cold war movie
about Russia. Lots of tundra, and little
mustached figures bundled up
in the corner, waiting
to do something. On skis.
Or dog sleds. A throw-back. Before
the Revolution? Before the Revolution.
Or not. I can't make it out
for the snow locked
back in that theater,
                      voices that blast
the eardrum
straight, such would-be whispers
of love. How is it
                    that time has
layers and layers,
some of which never move
or fill up. *Meanwhile:* a favorite word
any poem understands to be
snow's most legendary suggestion.
The second: melt.
                    The third: I need to
freeze first.

STUDYING HISTORY

Not the underwater goggles to see
great distances, not the *let's pretend*
of the museum's "Street of Yesteryear,"
its candy's single stripes in jars, life-sized
dummy at the counter,
stiff collar and apron, eyes skewed to retrieve
his blank good will. Nor is it
book after book of the same war
over remembered time, the old nun called it,
speeded up for the test. Wars of different
colors, weaves and counterweaves,
different surgical instruments, different
agonies via different
far-off blasts, different endlessly
pointless outcomes, different
tiny viruses ingesting
the lungs first, derailing trains there,
breath starting and stopping
at each smoky depot.
                        I sat at a desk
where we all sat. I opened
that book of flags. Once a woman took up
a whole half page, looming there,
middle of the 19th century, absolutely
glacial because happiness is momentary
and eternity is work, the camera
shrouded, laying
its slow black against white until her
terrible face found me.
                        Was that
childhood going on? That noise
in the background—half-starved, deranged bird,
half Hallelujah Chorus sung
by the whole town, bad tenors included? Ache
of cold metal on the playground,
one glove lost forever, night,

hours of it, caught
by a streetlight?
                    Which is simply
the past. In that book now, isn't it?
And a child is writing
his name in the flyleaf, under two or three
other names, the book already underlined,
half-forgotten. *Write clearly,*
write in ink, the teacher is saying.

AFTER THE MOON

eclipsed itself, the rumor of darkness
true, the whole radiant business
almost over, only a line,
an edge, like some
stray part of a machine
                                    not one of us
can figure any more:
what it thrashed or cut, what it sewed
quietly together, what it scalded
or brought back from the dead. After this,
I came inside to sleep.
                                    But it's the moon still,
pale run of it shaping
the door closed against the half-lit hall.
The eye is its own
small flicker orbiting under the lid
a few hours.
                                    Not so long,
bright rim,
giving up its genius
briefly, mountains under dark, craters
where someone, then no one
is walking.

A MUSICAL IDEA

At the second light, you turn, the boy tells me.
I turn. A musical idea. Turn then,
when a light in any house goes on.

Dark end of the day on the street. Dark
late afternoon in November.
In any kitchen—revealed: the hum

starts in the freezer, down
the lower shelves, takes the stove back
to its fire. The sink is an absence,

one tea-stained cup left to seed.
I live somewhere. But to walk away
is a musical idea. Because a corner means

make a profile to however once
you were. Once a child, I kept turning
full-faced into everything, never

saying a word. You like
to think that, my brother says. I heard you
plenty of times. And you were hiding.

OMNISCIENCE

To shrink down and not be small
> *but just to see again,* he said
> of the past, the past as broken mirror,
> as weird-looking stick
> because this was the woods,
> halfway through the hike.

To refrain from the cheesy, the self-serving, from
> *knowing too much.* That voice,
> his again. So there were rules. *But how can we*
> *know too much,* she said. *Memory,*
> she said, *come on, it's all about*
> *forgetting. Think of the things*
> *lost to make that box*
> *of odds and ends.* They

kept walking. Somewhere, a real road. They could
> hear it. He almost told her,
> you'll test me now. You'll ask me
> how long did it take
> to hold a pencil, to write the word
> *fabulous* or maybe just *dog*
> for the first time. And if he
> shook his head— See? she'd say,
> see? *I remember the fifth grade,* he said,
> *those endless afternoons, don't you?*

Not one, she said. They got quiet, the river
> on their left now, the water
> too low. The whole world
> needed rain. But she flashed
> on that strange little
> storefront in Oregon once,
> the counterman saying: why, there
> you are! I've been waiting a decade
> for you to walk in here.

Then she was telling it, outloud, in the air. *Probably*
a pick-up line, he said. *What*
were you? 20? 22? Sudden click
in her head, a double take, two
exposures, one picture,
the first shock of it back
from the photo lab:
and here I thought

it merely some brilliant bit of the novel
my life was writing. Did they pause?
Because I hear him about to say:
so you kept it, that's
funny. They walked on. A field
opened up. *Is that*
a song sparrow

or a white-throat? he said. *I can't remember,* she said, notes
rushing downward but three clear
hesitations before that great
blurring. It got darker,
crooked ash and ivy, an overgrown
path where I stopped.
Where the two of them
kept going.

NICE

I can be nice. I can put my body
flat, down straight, and pull
sleep from somewhere deep

in the brain, that no-weather
thing, that blank page-
after-page thing. I can be

nice enough and say nothing, drift
to the cool room under
a blanket, under all the things

I have to do. Count them. Count
forward or backward: glue
broken things, fill the feeder,

work for a living, make supper, go
anxious unto guilty unto
anxious, full circle. I can love

humankind. I can do that.
I can close my eyes on the bright
windows my neighbors have

framing their big TVs. I can understand.
I can be nice when others decide, steeling
myself, but not as well as my tiny

grandmother did, the tallest person
in the room for a moment. I can, mostly,
drive past Burger King, its *Good Luck*

Staci (oh, Stacy with an i!) *We Miss You!*
on whatever the marquee's
called now, be touched and sweetened

or nice enough not to notice. And bite
my tongue. Good doggy. Be nice now, be
nice. I can sacrifice muscle

and bone to sit longer, showing
interest (*show interest*, my mother warned
as we walked through any really large

set of doors). I know German has
a word, *nett*, for nice. I can put myself
in that net, drop down so close

to what is underwater
that the fish know me as small,
silent, as sleek and shiny as

they happen to be. And so
weightless there, blue
beyond thought. One would hardly

guess how nice it is, those fish
suspended next to me, their mouths
opening and closing.

SEVEN AUBADES FOR SUMMER

day one

I read the roof next door. I read
the shingles, their stony
overlap, the stubborn look
my grandmother gave me: *I won't*
walk that street. I hate
those people. But she didn't
say that. I was a child. And to protect
is to change the subject
and leave the wound, only
one of us
staring down and down. So it was
she clipped the brown glass
to her glasses and we
took a different route. Brick
sidewalk, weedy grass. The shrug
of a small town. And her steel,
a flash of it. One bird out there
can't get over his song. To repeat
is to remember. To remember is to go
on and on. *Anyway*, my husband
said this morning, throwing back
the sheet.

day two

No one take credit. *It came to me*
in a dream is all anyone
can say. The dream of two sparks
makes another spark. And if only
I could think beyond and more oddly, this
stolid whatever-it-is, this stanza

a room, just a figure in a doorway
about to leave
or to enter. It was my mother
come back to life, so much younger
as I slept, plotting herself
out of a marriage. So I finally
witnessed it, the moment she opened and closed
and opened. But how did it end?
My standing there, my wanting to . . .
And the sequel, her
splintered look of no and yes. And I was
the child who emptied to say
anything at all.

That's summer, isn't it? The earth turned
toward instead of away. It takes a whole night
to do that. *She's a busy little bee,* I heard
someone say yesterday, each word a stone
set down carefully, each weighing
a pound or two. I work on that, both
the acid and the praise. Nothing's simple,
not even the start of the day.

day three

Cars go either way up the street,
blue and dark green and red, white
and off white, dashes of color
that vanish under fabric—
someone patient, someone stitching.
And closer, those trees, conifers, both
of them older than I am, huge.
And if I find
grief in their shade this early, if I
find my own blurred self
cast on the ground there, a shape,
shadow, not the real branch
and shiver, what am I—a thief, a liar?
But I would. I'd steal
from those trees, how daylight comes
and throws them out of themselves
onto walkway and grass. I thought stain.
I thought locked-to-it, these
years and years.

day four

My brother on the porch once
in light like this, aiming his camera off its
sturdy tripod, black and big enough
to leave a sleeping baby in
who dreams without
language, without any past at all.
So he disappeared
inside its shroud, weird costume
in a miracle play, not the horse's head kept
for the pageant but a box that repeats
and stills, this dark he pulls over himself
to be no one the long moment. What
did the lens narrow to, if not—no—
the clematis purpling wildly
in its fretwork.

day five

Here is summer, said the light. Welcome to my hunger,
said the wren, trilling sideways and out. And the nuthatch, his
elegant gloom over everything is nevertheless
sweet. Shrink it down, make
it stay. Between leaf and leaf is wind
but only the leaf says so. Or both of them. Or all of them,
brief frenzy. I knew night
all night.

day six

If I skipped a day, would there be
a song? Let the cat do it, stretched
on the bed, sprawled against me, not wary
for once. Let the print of a print of a print
Doré once did
do it, there on the wall, angels in the dark
coming at me off a ship in those waters,
the 19th century endless and adrift
and never light enough to see. Let the three
doors of this room open to it. Let the laundry basket
overflow with it. Let the books piled
whichever way and too many
do it, cry *aubade,* cry
word no one knows anymore,
its little scheme to stop time
almost stopped. Let my tea
do it, a hit of milk, no sugar. Am I done
with this? Am I? Day that will pass
and not be remembered, lighter
than its air.

day seven

Trustees of the dark, I heard you voting
to adjourn, declaring yourselves
over and incompetent, no longer fit
to govern. I saw your cruise of a lifetime
dissolve past the shadowy dock, into last
as in last night, the wee hours, the lie-awake-
and-listen-for-chimes-across-town hours.
Five now, or six. I count them
out there, just a part of what's bigger—
branch and car door, bird quick or slow,
back to back, call and call, this
one thing after another, dizzy-sharp
then simply dizzy. Try closing
your eyes again. Try
those other things.

THE PARK IN NOVEMBER

could be part rain or part twilight
or it's a car pulling up. Late afternoon
not warm, not too cold.
It's *I haven't, I couldn't*. But a woman
sits in that car, a man there too,
a shadow coming down not a curse,
just rain with its nothing
to do in this shelter. It's damp
and nothing but benches cut
with a knife: the standard *fuck you* and so-
and-so *loves Julie* or *Mike* or *Chris W*, names
scratched inside nervous
little hearts, each a heat-sink, stupid
sudden-luck box, a wound
in reverse. I can't tell. Why would anyone
sit in a car like that? She's crying.
Or he could be crying. I see it.
I x-ray dusk. I'm a tragedy-seeking instrument
of—no, not light. Her hands on the wheel,
she's miles from here now. Rain,
the afternoon, those hardly-any-words
between them. I mean
nothing opens why she
stays up front, why he's over
into the back now. Why the car
is a room in a house
neither imagined. Why breath
goes white on a window if certain
things cannot be said.

RADIO

A box with music coming out of it—hard climb
of cello oblivious to the violin
secret, not quite
scheming. But the news,
bright here-it-is, then weather with its
rain and its colder.
                    And news again, bloody
flashes or warm fuzzies,
depending. Sure. Right. Because
the dream of making sense
is making shape. Alternating. Those shiny
transparencies that hypnotize and keep
the textbook heavy: bones
austerely dealt under the slippery
roadways of heart and deep stain, under a page
of skittery nerves, a tangle.
                          It's all a bloody tangle.
I follow the plug to the wall.
Give it a rest. The antenna pretends
there's a heaven. But I leave it on.
Because supper, because
dusk means something steaming
in a bowl. I wield a knife to the quick
of the cutting board.
                    Black box with knobs
whose mesh
leaks whatever human agony. Sometimes
a catch there, registered
by pause and pause. Hear that? Exactly
the weight of
insidious minus *roar* equals
no down to that
smaller *no.*

THE DOCTOR

I read bodies, she says. So I
show her what I was
given, trusted with, wake
up to, tell her where
and what, which arm or leg, which
ache near dawn,
the flash at the back of the skull,
a narrowing in muscle
or bone or nerve
that makes it a city suddenly
built so badly, so far
from the sea, first a rumor
then after, such photos
to carry about, tiresome
drone of travel there repeated
endlessly, variation
chilling to theme, news
that comes back as I try
to remember, to tell her
whatever. And she reads
with stethoscope and glove, a tiny
light for those dizzying
channels in the head, looking up
or into, locking my joints then
unlocking them slowly
or quick: look left—good—look
right, lie down, breathe
shallow, now deep. To say
braille would be putting it all
into dark. But what goes on
is mindless, brilliant
pulse where wrist
is most bluish, the skin a veil,
bones the thinnest shuttle
crossing, recrossing.
Her questions: how long? or

when-I-press-this and do you feel it
dull or sharp? And can she
believe me or this country
she's never seen, never been to?
Maybe it's familiar, this place.
She might know
the language, she might,
of its slow, well-meaning
citizens, most of whom don't want
to come out of their houses, ever.
Really, a simple quiet room
would do. And please,
a small to medium bowl
of something.

LIGHT ON FOUR SIDES

—Chicago, 1975

I always say: light on four sides.
I always say: amazing dreams there too.
In fact, count six rooms, that
corner apartment, Granville
crossing Lakewood, eight blocks from the water,
third floor so we could
overlook things: our sadness—no, not
sadness yet. Our hopelessness—no, we had
a small porch. The fourth side
opened out back, a porthole of light
to the up-down-sideway
fire escape, someone's laundry there like birds
about to wingspan off, and old men
driven out to their pipes
and cigars. Exquisite loneliness
on a summer night. There are joys
you keep to yourself.

I was always sleeping too much
in that place. Because to sink down into its depth
was to find things. The end of the world,
for instance. I did. I dreamt its shrieks
one night. I dreamt its tears. It was there
a woman stopped me, looking everywhere
but at me—*I've led a good life, haven't I?*
haven't I?—kept on, kept
almost screaming. But everyone
was about to scream
or screaming. And I waited there,
that ticking quiet right
before panic floods. I could
feel its rise—keeping it down, slow, to hold on,
thinking, no, I am invisible, I am
no one, I am not here, I'm
dreaming, for god's sake. Then so
abruptly, so sucked in—was it even

a thought?—*the world*
has ended before. (I swear to this,
to all dreams, the way they startle
and stay and enter the body
as oxygen carried in, to carry off
such dark). What does one do
when the world ends? Such a question,

so rational, so bloody British in the old-movie
matter-of-fact way. But it calmed me. It did.
Something to do now. How we think
we manage, all that next and next. Bury the books!
It came to me. Really, I had nothing
to do with it. The thought flashed, it burned
in my head: you bury the god-damn books!
(Forgive this line with chalk
I'm drawing. Forgive this *story.*)
The city library? I ran there.
In the dream I mean. I ran
to its rubble and ash. Gone! And still
smoking. Still some feeble
flame. So I found
another way, near that distant
heaving, the lake,
its shine oblivious to the end
of anything—or its beginning, for that matter,
—this blue gray given of my childhood,
of anyone's rush and release. Only I wasn't

for a minute original. Already they were at it—
whoever they were—in a line from library door
to graveyard beside it. (Forget real
typography. Forget there never was
a graveyard.) That library, in or out of dream,
on rocks, the lake's silver, gritty edge,
built for Mundelein, the Catholic college
my mother hoped
hopelessly I'd choose. Those human
shadows—dutiful, quick—digging up

coffins, lifting them from their concrete
encasements—is that what they're called?—
for books. To bury the books! Of course.

And the rest of us? *Us.* For now I had quietly
stepped into line and did what any
lost creature might do, dumbly, with passion: I took
the book given me and passed it
to the next outstretched hand. And the book
after that and the book after that
and so on and so on, deep into dream
and beyond it, to this remembering
right now: everything stacked and lowered
to be safe—the generous
and the silly, the wise, the small, even books
with their one thought fanned
too many pages, a trick of love and dogged
concentration. Zane Gray and Aquinas, Whitman
and Whittier and Cather, Lewis Thomas so his
Lives of a Cell would live
somewhere contained, multiplying
as we moved through whatever
awful light. That's the odd thing: *vapid*
next to *beautiful,* neighbor
to *humble* to *glibly holding forth*
to *forget everything!* to
forget whatever's left. No matter,
I told myself, no matter—all of it
the spirit life lifted
hand to hand, set down to be

cherished, to be kept dark.
We were sweating and squinting and not
one of us spoke. None of us. That's it,
that's all I have. I mean
happiness so deeply
surprises—not *no* turned *yes,* past
what to do, world ending
as it does. And it will. But this thing

so buried in us, that it has
any words at all. Which is to say,
I woke stunned. That's
what I brought back
to tell you.

II

THE BODY

has its little hobbies. The lung
likes its air best after supper,
goes deeper there to trade up
for oxygen, give everything else
away. (And before supper, yes,
during too, but there's
something about evening, that
slow breath of the day noticed: *oh good,
still coming, still going . . .*) As for
bones—femur, spine,
the tribe of them in there—they harden
with use. The body would like
a small mile or two. Thank you.
It would like it on a bike
or a run. Or in the water. Blue.
And food. A habit that involves
a larger circumference where a garden's
involved, beer is brewed, cows
wake the farmer with their fullness,
a field surrenders its wheat, and wheat
understands *I will be crushed
into flour and starry-dust
the whole room*, the baker
sweating, opening a window
to acknowledge such remarkable
confetti. And the brain,
locked in its strange
dual citizenship, idles there in the body,
neatly terraced and landscaped.
Or left to ruin, such a brain,
wild roses growing
next to the sea. The body is
gracious about that. Oh, their
scent sometimes. Their
tangle. In truth, in secret,
the first thing
in morning the eye longs to see.

ST. FRANCIS IN WINTER

Snowbound, St. Francis in the iris bed, snow
making a little cap for his stony head.
He's maybe a foot and a half, smaller
from the kitchen window, his thoughts
an inch wide, an inch deep. His furrowed brow—
the half-master of concrete who poured him, then
shook him from his mold nevertheless
narrowed by hand each line of worry there.
Snow peaks on his shoulders, palest
drift last night, a veil of it
over the streetlight when I looked out late
in the no-moon dark. It came down.
It kept coming. I didn't think
solace, seeing that. I didn't think
St. Francis-over-the-frozen-iris-oh-
vast-strange-nonhuman-
sounding because it was
near-sleep washing
the house away and we were about
to turn and walk upstairs.
Morning now, the dream of not
being here over, St. Francis
more alone than he's ever been. Kingdom
of patience, kingdom of his badly-
chipped outstretched hand. So cold
out there, not even a bird, not even its
splintered call, the yard
white, its enormity absolute
and small, everything St. Francis knows
but keeps forgetting.

LADDER AGAINST A HOUSE

So someone climbed it. But now
it's dark. Now it's neither street
nor curb, sidewalk,
yard, neither weed nor grass.
But this thin outline,
ladder against *house,* trace
of the will to go up or
no, earth is
the welcoming place. I'm walking by.
Or imagining I walked here.
And stopped to see it's not
an invitation, no lit window
hovering to receive it, nothing
at this hour to be bolted
or scraped or primed or
painted. It might be
wood, once a pine in a narrowing
swatch of pines. As for the rungs,
how an oak stood
years, slowly shifting into the great arc
of its falling. Summer. There was
such a leaf stained
by the next leaf, cooler in those
woods, men shouting to be
heard over the blistering
racket of their saws.
I'd climb higher. But the tree's
lost all contact with its story.
That's the thing
about transformation. *There are*
worse fates, it did not
even vaguely say to itself.

LUNCH

The zoo. So one thinks up from
the amoeba, way ahead to one's great-grandchildren
someday or no day. Then back where old
photographs live, those minutes
locked in the ice
of someone's remembering, some uncle
with a camera. But the zoo—here!—
is very matter-of-fact: warm bodies (monkeys,
zebras, any moving thing
with beak, with feathers) versus
the flashing cold and/or hot ones: the bite-the-dirt-
for-all-we-do-wrong ones
or the soft-bellied frog or the salamander flattened,
shrunk, puffed out, its legs, arms,
sweet little claws completely
not a snake, having lured no one and nothing.

I was saying: consider the metal bars. To keep
such wonders in, to keep us—smaller wonders—out.
Almost noon, some uniformed someone
turns up with bananas, seeds,
fetal pigs, apples, the works. How not
to love this guy?—his trusty
indifference, his all-right-another-day-of-it
shrug and off-key whistle. The animals
look up. *Something is about to happen.* Food

does that. In this saddest of worlds, think
lunch! and an ocean of hope
rides over us. Is it hope? And too cheap? This
metaphor filling the moment? the mind?
the life finally and exactly? I mean
the guy's coming closer, the one
with a bucket. And a shovel.

PIANO WITH DISTANCE

I guess I could play it.
Sound in my head coming

the same time my hand
does something. Or before

I hear a thing. This thing grand
and black, sideways-languid

as an island you'd approach
from the air, big, forever

torturing its spun wires inside,
stretched low or high. And they

break—when? Just past
the most lofty, squeezed out, my

chipping-away-with-a-hairpin
note. We used to make

thunder as kids, booming
in the lowest register our brief

stories of utter disaster. And then
the high quick fall of rain—

supposed to be soothing. It was
mindless—that clink clink clink.

What can I say? We were
easily pleased by the famously

unoriginal. Ours
was a spinet. I never learned right.

I never really learned though
my teacher, a genius, one

Mr. Schwartz, inch
by inch brought

every other instrument
in the fabulous world

to my lessons—violin, clarinet,
gleaming small bicycle wheel

of French horn I heard
to my left turning over

and under my unthinkable
measures. But the oboe took me

right out: goodbye little living room,
goodbye St. Bartholomew's,

Cornelia Avenue, Chicago, 1959.
At last!—Mr. Schwartz

forgot me plugging away
at my minuet, he oboe-lost to circle

an impossible planet yet to be found
by some trick of math or

discovered for real and given a name,
adrift where it wasn't cold, wasn't

dark but it got darker. Isn't he
something? my mother always

said later. So I included her too—
me! eking out my terrible Mozart,

she way back in the kitchen
levitating, oh somewhere

in that hour, secret
whoever she was.

HELLO

And I look—where? But it's a stranger
on a cell phone. A chiming

rush of words, her *are you sure?*
and *no, don't tell me that.*

I'm back to unlocking
the car. Day like any other.

Because one must look away. She's
whispering emphatically

everything about last night, what she
remembers slowed to a standstill

right there on the sidewalk. I fix
on a robin somewhere, a half-hearted

che er ily—he stops, starts—*che er ily.*
He's lost the middle kingdom

of his song. She's almost
crying. She can't believe anything

some voice through no wire at all
is telling her. A camera

on me, you'd see exactly
anyone, carefully oblivious,

doggedly clicking taut the seatbelt,
adjusting the rearview mirror.

What is private in public
idles there, invisible. O worm

under the rose. How old is this rule?
Honor the first to know.

SIMPLE MACHINES

The spoon, for instance, just
suggests in its small half moon, the size
of a good swallow, its weight
the first bare counter-weight
against a thing so huge.
                              Hunger, a machine too—

red light switched on
to alert, alert, the humming
begun in any
similar steelbox.
                              The fork makes

further distinctions, the world
not to be gathered but seized, not
invited in
but pierced, dragged along. So we
absorb, refuel,
                  reset brain, heart,

the mercurial point-of-view
shifting with each bite, finally
omniscient now: oh, all of us sated, every last
glad living thing.
                              The bowl—just

a larger spoon for the little spoons
to visit, grow inspired, rising
to whatever lips. The plate—a white or blue
expanse, the dream we have
to the horizon line
                              at the edge of the table

where even the most unsinkable ships
might vanish because the world
is flat via the eye's most clever

first machinery. Everyone but Columbus
knew that. And the knife.
                                    Better not
think of the knife, its blade
turned in for the moment, so spare in its
beauty, between spoon
and plate, resting too quiet
in the shade there.

RELICS

I saw a bone in plastic, the card
sewn in a circle around it,
the empty-eyed ecstasy
of the veiled figure
in a painting, printed in a factory,
hand-sized. St. Whoever's

little something. It led
to light. And cost several dollars—
how much?—in the dusty street,
rough translation of so many lire.
I suspect one chicken
died an awful death, and gave up
her tibia—do they even have them?

But a first class relic
is a first class relic, whatever
the creature, ie: *the*
body part. (Think of St. Catherine's
head in Sienna, her heart in Rome—
or am I reversed on this?—that ache and cry
must still carry on, each to each, head
to heart, how many miles? We took
that train but did not count.)

And second class relics? *All things*
the saint touched. My perennial example:
the road-kill glove. Or mittens
we took, strays
crusted on snow banks, stepped
to slush. Lopsided tiny reindeer or where
some cross-stitching mother
eked out stars. To come in cold
to the line of them

tacked up, their wave after wave, every
last nothing. To be
in that hall. Before that,
to open a door.

night somewhere. Maybe he's
singing, if you could see it

or be it, barely-there growl
on the record. Small givens

get lost, brief rabble
under snow, final leaf

upon leaf. Under *for sure*,
not so sure. Those leaves

in splinters, all edges, can walk
when you walk, clinging to a boot.

Under sleep, dream or no dream.
I don't remember movies, my favorite

disclaimer. Under movies,
the premise of dark, a looking

out of and into, the screen
always too large or we get

used to it. Under bigger than life,
that small thing that

started things. A laugh in the cold,
empty distance of winter

carries, one says, *it carries*.
Under that, this wish for a chair,

a cup, a window, the other side
of such weather, the great

company of being
lonely alone the point

of all music. Glenn Gould too
human at Bach, low-watt

rushing just under our own
screening anything out.

HAPPINESS: THREE DEFINITIONS

1.

Can you be too happy? Put some
in a box. Tape it. Put it on that
shelf over there. Come Sadness,
little dog no one likes
but you're sweet, you are,
in your way. So I go
to the woods with that dog.
I don't teach it anything. Not *heel,*
not *fetch*, not
protect me from monsters.
He hardly looks back at me,
never brings me
a stick to throw past him
to the river. The river
doesn't shine in these woods. Doesn't
make a sound. There's an old
washing machine in it. A couple
of shoes. Or three. No match
for any other, one with laces
adrift like some languid
sea creature, tentacles bleached,
wayward, not caring a bit
if the fisherman comes with his net
or not. I'm that happy.
I don't care either.

2.

Which leads to a question. Can
happiness make you stupid? (I love
stupid, said Stupid. What? said Smart.
But that's a different story.) The world
looks great without

sepia, without eye trouble, the moon,
one moon. And all this blinding
daylight, just what we wanted, yes?
Question: do you relish
or endure? Two curious
adjustments on the lens. Or three:
it depends, you said or I said, not sure
what to fix for dinner. (Did we
remember limes? cilantro?
coconut milk?) It's just that, how
stupid to *qualify* stupid, said
Stupid. Or was it Smart at the window,
talking to no one in particular, squeaking
the balloon into the shape of a duck
or a windmill.

3.

In fact, things happen
in threes, said everyone after the second
disaster (those strokes, that trainwreck—you
name it—an earthquake, a flood). We
eyed the room, each other, checking
the door—is it locked for the night?
Then I slept and dreamt people
walking in lines, carrying their picket
signs: *no third thing!* I could
belabor this. I could say as my
long ago friend did: how do you get there?
First you go there! Then laugh
myself sick. Or tell that dog:
no, Sadness. You have to stay home.
You can't nuzzle the leaves
with me all afternoon. But the way
he looks up, out of focus,
so eye to eye.

MINUS MINUS

I go to Bach to rearrange
my brain. Am I generous?

Make me mean. Am I addled?
Smart. Or reverse, reverse.

My mean turns
sweet. My knowing

whatever small thing
is *thing,* is infinitely

small. Veil of light
that repeatedly

repeats: *bike quick,*
hear it *summer,* hear it

afternoon. Because
The Art of the Fugue, each

meticulous inch
and leap and no future

this fierce, every bit of dappled
shade in there

and here, on the bike path:
To be the only

human thing for all
these minutes! The only

human thing
isn't human. Isn't

isn't. Says who? Says
such intricate

machinery, brain's
crosswork and firing past

air, past water or leaf
going under, falling

lost minus found,
back back minus

nub. Break of day, mend
of night. Radiant

here and in spite of, lie
down. Be this dark.

AT THE SAME TIME

An annotated list: rain, not
rain (proof: I was squinting)

or everyone grinning
in the photograph. Forget

cancer, the little strokes arriving
one knuckle at a time, now

or not yet, dark ghostings
in the side vision: his, hers,

yours, mine. At the same time, nothing
then something left on the porch,

a can of coconut milk, a note
in green ink, a package

of spices for *laksa*, soup
of the gods. *We are not gods*

but I talk to one, the huge nun
breathed up, all of her pitched

over us, filling the room, fierce
smile that frowned. She was

way too big to be human.
We were small, the beginning

of human. *See? Close your eyes,*
she flooded us again.

THINK OF THE WORDS

lost to a short pencil, words like *milk,*
eggs, celery, gone to the library, I
fed the cats all flying through it,
using it up. And that eraser coming down,
those second thoughts, that how-do-you-spell-that,
those changes of heart—serious, be gone!—when
a line drawn through whatever word
would do. When a single shoe
appears in the street, think
of the scramble. Someone lifted, carried off,
someone running, someone that
distraught, that drunk or
indifferent, that something. (Who's right?
my brother asked my mother
before any overwrought TV.) No, erase.
Delete. If we revisit
the pencil, I'd write a few more words
to wear it down. *I'm all worn out,* I heard
again and again through my childhood. Three
generations after supper, such
mulling for the night. Worn out? I thought
of a tire—you can't get a penny
in its tread—or pants out at the knee, shirts
thin at the elbow, never who
we really are, life that
seems unstoppable. Never the small,
hard eraser at the end of it.

IN A FRAME, IT MATTERS

A laugh is genuine
or not. So we goofed around
until we forgot
the camera there. What was our

name for this? Please: we need
a record of childhood, of young
adulthood, of that vast cloud
in the middle, of the days

one is grateful to eke out
in old age. Outside the world
impossibly revives itself without anyone
looking at it. Even the squirrel knows

night is a darkness with a string of lights
at either end. But where did he
put them? The hard gifts of summer
and fall. In the earth somewhere.

Brain that can't remember exactly
but he's back there,
winter-hungry. It was here, wasn't it?
And we looked like this.

ALL NIGHT

Night took red
out of the garden, took the blue
of course, took
the pink in spite of moonlight,
yellow, in spite of the stars.

Took our sense
of the day, how the car
fixed itself—a miracle. How
painting that room
did us in—hey, we're old!
you said. So supper
was quick: eggs, some
decent bread. How we thought
to walk anyway but
after we ate, not before, passing
those kids with their late
lemonade stand. A night cap!
one shouted as we
got closer.

There were other things. Night
took the war
and lied in happier ways
a few hours: *you're right,*
you just dreamt such wretchedness.
Not even the word
wretchedness because in the real
nature of night, it was
never mentioned. I had a dream last night,
a friend told me years ago. But I slept
right through it. Remember?
Sleeping like that? And before night?
Three or four of us
still up, talking intently
around the table in the kitchen.

THE DRAWING MANUAL

—after Nicolaides

The shadow of my hand
as I write this—*there is no
such thing as shadows,*

I remember reading. But now
the lamp is a moon and my hand
a cat in the flower bed, its

ready-to-leap burning
darker there. *Where light
does not get through is*

called a shadow, I read again.
But the tip of my pencil
meets its narrow ghost

only in this semi-gloom. Pause
or go on, gauzy overlay
sticking, stuck to my hand.

What I thought
I might write: "a day once
in its onceness, the onceness

in any day lived through."
Such nonsense! My knuckles
cast their shroud

on paper as I keep
this curious pace, each word
swallowed by my own

quick spill. The hand is
a hero, dragging its
small war behind it, flat now

and gray and *if you must choose,*
ignore the shadow
and draw the form. I imagine

he said that many times before he
wrote it, those students
puzzled, looking up. No,

it's a window
throwing his underworld
shape to the floor.

SNOWFALL IN G MINOR

Overnight, it's *pow!* The held note
keeps falling. And only seems
slow. Because it's just
frozen rain, what's the big deal? the checker
in Stop and Shop told me.
                                    Save warmth
like stamps. The fade of their color
in the 1920s. Airmail. The pilot with his
skin-tight goggle helmet on his
miniature head could be
snow-blind.
                           All heads are small. Mine's
lost as a thimble
in this weather. Where
a finger should be and be
sewing, every thought
I ever thunk.
                         Just this word
thunk. Never used.
It lands, noisy
metal in a bucket. That's
the last of it. No echo
for miles of this
                         snowfall—as in
grace, fallen from,
as in a great height, released
from its promise.

AMBITION

One cat. I hear her out there.
Then a door. And then

her name: *Hannah, Hannah!*
My neighbor come alive

this early. The cat returned
from the night without

damage. The same night
I dreamt others stepped forward

to explain or to thank,
the public voice at the front

of the room, words
through a small microphone

clipped to a lapel. Everyone
so busy. Inside my quietude,

an uneasiness. Inside that,
another stillness at the table

like the great past before
I was born, or the future when I'm

out of here for good, a thing
muffled in me, slow,

turned back to a seed
in a cup. And water for it

out of reach. And a window
over there. But the others

were kind. In the dream,
they passed me

the plate of sweets. They
returned whatever face

I gave them—puzzled,
amused, intent, disbelieving—

the same look, honed to meet
my eye, however

briefly. Hot tea now, almost
light. The cat come home

without damage. I didn't think
to leave, but I woke.

MAP

The lines aren't really boundaries, not
the edges of anything, the woman said.
I followed her hand,
                             point A to point C.

B was all blue
and she skipped it. C was a dot
with a circle around it,
                             a city, voices,

everyone talking at once,
a cacophony. So quiet in the car
before I turned on the motor,
                             map on the seat

open, a map so sure
of itself. And rivers,
no color at all, jagged,
                             indifferent to land,

cross-angled, irrational
though of course, they
move toward a wide place,
                             a delta, slow

magnet, such water,
an ocean. I could sit staring for hours
like that, I tell myself now,
                             for hours,

an exaggeration that might
please a child who does
almost nothing for hours.
                        But it did. It took

hours to cross, only
ten inches long in my car, ten inches
wide, square of busy
                    exactitude. What I love—

the swatches of silence,
an inch, two inches, a bare spot,
pale yellow where
                    nothing had happened.

In fact I drove
through a universe, fields,
their intricate
                    wildlife of insects

and beans, civilization of mice
and moth and corn, windfall,
the great trees
                    finally over in an instant.

FEBRUARY

That sparrow on the trash again, one
leg missing, he
alights and drops down, alights
in this cold, and crooked,
drops down again though he could
fly. He has to, most of the day
I imagine, into its
exhaustion, those moments he
finds a window sill or a patch
of old leaves under some
overhang, his one leg, good wire,
pulled under him, feathers
puffed out—swollen thing, ridiculous—
for warmth. All the lives I
might have had: this one,
oh, this one.

III

WHAT GOD KNEW

when he knew nothing. *A leaf*
looks like this, doesn't it? No one
to ask. So came the invention
of the question too, the way all
at heart are rhetorical, each leaf
suddenly wedded to its shade. When God

knew nothing, it was better, wasn't it?
Not the color blue yet, its deep
unto black. No color at all really,
not yet one thing leading to another, sperm
to egg endlessly, thus cities, thus
the green countryside lying down
piecemeal, the meticulous and the trash,
between lake and woods
the dotted swiss of towns along
any state road. Was God

sleeping when he knew nothing? As opposed
to up all night (before there was night)
or alert all day (before day)? As opposed to that,
little engine starting up by itself, history,
a thing that keeps beginning
and goes past its end. Will it end, this
looking back? From here, it's one shiny
ravaged century after another,
but back there, in a house or two: a stillness,
a blue cup, a spoon, one silly flower raised up
from seed. I think so fondly of the day
someone got lucky
and dodged the tragedy meant for him. It spilled
like sound from a faulty speaker
over an open field. He listened from
a distance. *God-like,* any one of us
could say.

THE TIN HOUSE

Some days the mystery is familiar,
every shade pulled down,
not sun-wrapped or fire-thrown, that
tin house I walked by, for instance,
running as a kid runs, taking a stick
to its corrugated, sea-sick surface,
the *blip blip blip*, thinking so little
of the old man inside who
peed in a can and threw it out back.
My brother and I, that bit
of cruelty. Do it over. Slow this down.
It wasn't mystery
but childhood which never blinks
even if the sun's too hot, even now
when I think of him hearing us,
two brats laughing, about to pick up
those ancient weapons, broken off
branches thick enough
to run the length of that house
straight up from the street,
his hearing us say *is he in there?*
if we ever thought to say that. He stood
quiet, not moving, a gradual
thickening, only a shape in a window cut
out of tin or a darkness
at the glassed-in door. He was waiting,
I think now, for it to be over, this
small injustice. Or he was waiting for us
to grow up, for the moment my brother
would turn to me—*I feel
really bad about that*—both of us
finally walking there, not a thing
in our hands, nothing to him,
less than nothing.

THE GARDEN

So many ways to call shapes
out of a dying world. Be a snake,
said the snake to the girl
drawn out of the rib, the garden
too beautiful to be noticed as she
stands there still, long enough
to want something, something
else. So the beginning
of all stories, the culling

of expanse and rest, quick
rise in wind then
the hush of *about*
to happen. Digression isn't
always evasion. She digressed
in wonder, watching that snake, such
intelligence, I suppose.
There are options, the snake said,
to this beauty. What

beauty? she thought, or felt in her chest.
Did Eve have language? Did she say that
out loud? Aren't words the curse
that comes later, our daily gruel, mouthful
by mouthful, a little milk, some sugar
to please ourselves, to think ourselves
so astonishing? But she
knew it. To be exact, she wanted
to know, sudden
heat and stirring: police tape
cordoning off where blood makes
a trail to suggest
the last breath, a small
stained fascination. Eve
hypnotized: oh, the strange and not-here,
not-of-this-garden, not really. I could be,

she thought, or simply *me* and *my hands*
moving toward something, a wish
all at once to be
covered, to be secret, to have
a thought like no other.

And what did the snake
dream, this snake that could talk
in this garden that never was
but marks our fate? Before falling into dust,
forced to love filthy water
and the highest grass concealing bright
as the moon its cold side, its
dark side, the snake was
dazzling. Story
that never happened. The snake was
human. *Over here, closer*, he said
to the girl come out of the rib.

THE DEER

are tentative. Of course. To be an animal
is to watch. Is to think
about eating all the time. I watch them
be so watchful. My window
takes them one by one through trees
winter strips down
to a few species.
                        When I saw the deer,
I was beginning to type, not
it came to me, full of: I made this.
But two or three were smaller than the others.
And all so thin,
each forgetting for a moment, a head turned
or down to the ground. Then the rush
to catch up. Maybe
a mother among them.
I'm hopeless about kinship, which cousin, which way
the bloodline hollows out a life
and connects us back
to a pin dropped once in a field
or in woods like these.
                        The poem to be typed—
I forgot the window's job
is to disappear. The deer,
just there, drawn
by a leaf or two left to the weather, a bud in its
vague dream of some future—

                        mid-sentence. Stop.
They're gone. Because beauty's
not generous, isn't anything
but its passage.

TELEPATHY

On the bike path—boys
too big for their bikes, outgrowing them,
hunched over the handlebars,
silly above the shrink-down wheels.
And middle-aged guys in their perfectly
stretched colors—red, bright yellow—
not a wrinkle in their
pitched-ahead pose on this new thing,
a cross between a racer
and a mountain bike.
                            But the boys,
they're all over the place—no helmet, of course—
and their knees splay out, too long-legged
for their little bikes. They squint.
They jumble up the path and love
their threat to me, coming at me,
careful not to see me.
                            And some of those men,
whatever day at the office
behind them, have no face at all.
Or do they? Only the dark
of their glasses, the jaw line
just so and distant. And maybe I'm just so
unfair. But *I'm your age!*—I want to shout—
remember our pathetic-sweet
kindergarten class? We took naps. We drank
milk with a straw. And then what? Years
of burn and rage. And so—
how did you vote? I don't even
want to know.
                            Here, these boys
practice happiness
with their bad lot: a bike too small?
A rousing *so what!* in summer's

late afternoon. I believe
in telepathy. *Don't
go to this war,* I think hard
as they pass.

WINTER

I dreamt of. And you were.
And our boy was a boy. And you and he
were putting up flags, a rope of them
in his room. The Tibetan kind:
earth equals yellow, white equals ether,
all of it for good and good, luck and luck,
the genius of that, you standing
at the rope's one end, our boy
at the other. The dream's genius.
Or winter's. Both of you
careful, how the flags draped
in the window, a small room
with its ceiling bent. And I was
an arrival because
I am here, years later. You almost
saw me. Oh the pull
of that rope—*Wake up. Be there.*
I dreamt of. And you were.

Because *winter*, I think. Or because
my *here* to your *not-here.*
Or because we are older. I could put on
my glasses, but I don't.
I could put on my boots, but I do not.
Snow is water frozen
sleepless, back to its habit of
expansion and contraction. It can't stop
and that it began at all
is blurring. So deep in dream,
I see it fall. See it
like the field at night takes light
cold from the sky, goes huge
and pale, set adrift against the far dark
rim of trees. I walk
beside it, not a companion, the simplest
element, one note held down, piano

of pure imagination, until the hand tires.
Trees that stop counting, earth
that opens to
any invention. Lost room of it
I dreamt of. And you were.
And our boy. The earliest day
in it. Careful. A rope
of flags, the ceiling bent. Green
was for wind. The pull
of that rope. Or the red one,
given to fire.

LEARNING TO READ

I don't remember learning to read, no—
not how each letter equaled one weird
disembodied sound. Maybe I wasn't that
crazy at first about two and two
making three or four, a gulp—a whole word—
then to the dogged slippery end of it, period.
But the exclamation point. That one.
It startled up, little ball and bat,
a jump in tenor, a welling-up
fast. Or the question mark, a hook
and its afterthought dropped into the sea,
broken off, some bit of a thing
floating there in the last half second.
As in that whispered *what? are you*
kidding? Small change in key,
amazed flashing its blue-green simply
out of amazement.

So I watch my friend's son
sound out words. Nikolas slowly taking his *b*
into *bread*, his *so* turning north into *soup*,
his *caaaa* hits its *t* and grows fur, is lithe
and purrs. Sound into thing. Thing into
this creature coming across the porch. My eye
holds it. I pick it up. Name it wildly
as my old cousin did: her *Tweeples,* her
On-e-po, her who-could-forget
Ughsome. I'm only saying

all praise to the question mark, the period,
any exclamation released breathless
at its point. Maybe this is
a love poem. Add the ellipsis which goes on
and on, holding its one true note
in a fade. But not fading. That anything
means and *is!* Nikolas watching someone

call to her children on the page, then all that
getting in the car. Years pass.
But here's a day of it
in the story, the hour of the swimming lesson.
He sounds that out in the dazzle
where they're poolside now, grinning, ready
to leap. *We-et.* Then faster—*Wet!* He's radiant.

YES LOVES NO

in its heart of hearts. Yes, so cheerful,
but looking for a little shade
in secret, ie: the underside
of a leaf is
almost interesting, its veins
delicate, crossing and recrossing,
a silent, stark
busyness, as in *who knew?* as in
and all this time. Because Yes remembered
the way to the graveyard and loved
to give directions, loved even how
No kept not getting it, not turning right
at the first right or even the second, how No
got too drowsy to drive and pulled over, Yes
smiling *I understand* but saying
I would think grief
would keep you awake. Bright nail
in the coffin and all that?
No, said No, going invisible then: Yes isn't
a bully, not really. Yes just wants
to get to the graveyard,
say certain things out loud, leave the potted marigolds
to the weather. *Well,* said Yes, *at least it's*
not raining. So by the side
of that road rarely traveled, Yes and No
sat quietly together, a few
minutes, I think. I timed them: maybe
a whole half hour, the tree shrouding them, an oak,
huge and riddled with rot. Yes dozing too
but oddly, eyes open. How can you
sleep like that? No wanted to say,
glancing sideways, quick.
And Yes, straight ahead, loved
those doubtful kisses.

IN THE WOODS: A SUITE

—Norton Island, Maine

I.

All right, I pledge to the pine
what small wonder I can muster.
Even then, a certain quiet takes
the woods. The optic nerve
can be perfectly awake, pressed back
into trance. Or so I watched
the Whirling Dervishes once, thinking
this never happens
in real life. But real enough,
that life—whatever moments,
an hour or two, sitting
in those cheap nosebleed seats,
so high it was a tiny
chain reaction, not quite
nuclear down there. What's
a dervish? my friend asked
after several minutes, from her
own splendid coma.

2.

Whatever was between
Dickinson and that fly: I want it.
So I'm very still, my fly
making its rounds around the cabin.
Its bad radar has it kissing
walls, bouncing off the ceiling.
I know. Everyone gets tired though
the pines put their limbs out
pretty much straight, keep
them there, day and night, a very
large exception. I think what it is
to be anything not human. Or how long

it's been afternoon, hours now.
Or how light only pleases
when there's enough shade
in it. And the fly. I forgot
about the fly.

3.

Somewhere out there, those crows
won't shut up. Maybe they can't. And then
they do. Which is why the thrush—I think
it's a thrush—comes out
from underneath with its weird
echoy thing, huge now but—*plaintive,*
my mother might have said.
Like the moment, a week from her death,
I put the earphones on her
in the hospital bed, Brahms, the first
piano trio—that cello, that rare violin—where
out of such fury something
narrows and goes deep. *What is it,*
she said, tearing up—the first time
in hours her speech was clear—*what
is it about music?*

4.

In the dark of these woods, rich
loam scent and buzz. In the dark of a car,
no moon, only the dash lit up. In the dark
of a box the cat finds to love, circling,
hidden as sleep. Or the moth's dark, where
wool disappears. Of childhood there,
wet scarves in the classroom, radiator
steam, rain dark and snow dark, past
afternoon. In the dark
of old engravings, the ancient mariner

asleep on the deck, intricate lines
make sky, make endless the sea that
has always been endless, and the few gulls,
their darkness is flight. In the dark
of a closed hand, a coin there or a stone
or a key. The door takes
it dark, small turn and a click
and a quiet. And that
house, oh that house, before
any light claims it.

HALF MORNING SONG

I'm sorry for the men who shovel the new layer of street
out of trucks, for my distrust of their certainty, their
get-on-with-it cheer. I'm sorry for my hands
in my pockets, for such solace I need, easy
and cheap. I'm sorry the day begins rotely,
that I can't hear the smallest trumpet. Sorry
my grandmother came alive again
at the end of my mother's life, my mother
so frantic then: *what is she eating? we have
to get groceries*, untangling herself, trying
to bolt out of bed. I'm sorry for the thin lip
of light this morning under the shade.
Sorry for the dark left behind. I'm sorry
about my brother's back: may it go straight and be
healed. May its flashing red turn violet
then blue. I'm sorry already
for my next complaint, my next tiny
panic not even a thought, not even a seed
or a twig though its tree
might be the elm doomed
since my childhood. Now I'm sorry for any
prophecy come true, this whole sorry litany
so close to complaint. Sorry sorry for the trellis leaning
sideways in the yard, the gate
too hard to latch, the bird house stuffed,
three summers of nests abandoned
and used and used to the third power, however
blessed that might be. I'm sorry
the sky is weeping this morning, though it's
raining. I'm told over and over,
it's raining.

ELEVATOR

Lower floor. And it's all about
standing there at a bus stop with maybe
my fidgety brother, years before
or alone, years of no car, when living
in a city meant patience, repeatedly
looking up the street. Without metaphor now,
I'm here, on the linoleum
of the great university, looking up
at numbers going red
and ascending. And that sound—wind tunnel
in the wall, this thing of vertical passage
between realms, between where I am
and where I must, between here and up there
on another floor where people
open envelopes right into the trash,
nodding *I know exactly what*
you mean, people meaning to tell
a roomful that Henry James was a genius
of the edgy compound sentence, ditto
Jane Austen of those big
houses, low fire in the grate
lost, after the fact, occasional
tickertape floating lightly to earth
on the English countryside.
Third floor. Fourth. Every stop
stops to the buzz of a fake floor
flush to the real floor rooted
on girders, the door opening to disgorge—
to disrobe, my brother might have said. Entry
into the next world for whatever stalwart
travelers come so far or so slightly,
straight up or straight down. And now it's
down. It's coming down slow
and slowly. I have time.
I can lean my forehead
against the cool metal: this

blip, sweet riff off the main music,
arteries and veins
in that darkness, rush
and pull of something saved from
must-I-live-forever-on-this-floor?
Thick ropey wires with never
enough give to move without bolting, this start
and stop that will be legend one day: *there once was*
a thing called an elevator. And the odd
graphic on the computer screen
will show a few strangers crowding
the smallest room
in the building, looking straight ahead,
shuffling sideways to make space
for the young woman, the exhausted
baby in her arms, child who
cries with such spirit. I hear it now, my ear
against the closed doors, something
unearthly, not human yet,
filtering down the shaft, distant
such weeping, the way stars
are muffled on cloudy nights
then reveal themselves, barely,
who they were
so many light years ago.

SPRING, IN FIVE PARTS

1.

Here's paper. Here's ink
in a steady line through the pen
in my hand. Here's the word
word and *here* and *hand*.
Can you think about thinking?
Can you take whatever passes there,
the shredded postcard delivered anyway,
pieced together out by the curb
in a truck, and taped? Thought like
a gene come down through the pool,
medieval moment, the bright, sweaty Renaissance,
every painter straining toward a ceiling.
Then into that river world, a new continent,
swift way from here to there, trees
in the distance or too close and you can't
see a thing. He was really a composer, the poet said
about the poet. He kept rewriting those lines
the way a composer hears things.
Tinkering dark, I thought, up to—not light.
It was a major key. Or the reverse, the utter
reverse of the angle. It drops into shade,
sinks back and back, not even
remembered anymore, those trees,
that continent.

2.

We were girls, high girlhood, fifteen
or sixteen. And the nun
not much older in that ordinary school
once a novitiate, not then, not
when we stood there in spring, the grounds
wooded and terraced, the light bulbs
bare, hung by their cords.
The hallway bent
to a spray of new light, three of us
talking to her, the young woman in those
black robes still—Vatican II
only a wish, a start. Her face
so like our faces, quickened and blank
by turns, opened and closed, curious, then
just-standing-by. And the religious life,
she called it, this thing she
stepped into thinking *world so
perfect*. She sounded like
singing, low note and no note. Or sadly—
was it sad?—her sudden
old to our young, her inside to our outside.
But I forgot, she said, *when you go anywhere,
you bring yourself.*

3.

I knew exactly. And then
I didn't. Was there a porch
in all this? Was there a house?
Light waxing out there, then
waning. A cat
slow and fragile and mean
and sweet by turns. He quickened
to a mouse, but only
a false one, fattened by catnip
and full of sewn seams. Days
unwind themselves. It's Monday,
then Friday, a lot of walking
in between, a lot of riding
in the car. A lot of spoon to mouth,
a lot of talk talk talk. I could, I suppose.
I mean I can, I said, agreeing.
Really, it's the cat at night, finding
that mouse again. A toy mouse, but he's
thrilled. Thrilled. I hear him
in the dark, his communion.

4.

There are questions. Does the bird
see the feeder first? Or does his hunger
find it? It's full, then empty
in less than two days. Their singing
doesn't change the subject. A flock
cleans it out. That would mean
sparrows or crows. Not the rare coupling,
nuthatch or cardinal.
                              Which is only to say,
it's spring. The lettuce barely
fringe in the raised bed, days you closet
winter coats back to their dark, when you
think about dragging screens
from the basement.
                        Think about—
An abruptness, right now. Dawn
eats night earlier these mornings.
Dreams stranger: old houses
left behind by the dead,
                              nothing unchanged
in the kitchen, not the model train
set up along the ceiling's edge,
not the scorched pots,
the dented spoons. To keep or not
to keep. Not that I know
what to care about, what to cast away.

5.

So shade overtakes the pond for an hour.
Part of the pond. Part
of the hour. I'd know my place
on the water, my hands
however awkward, the other side
looming up, closer
with every bad stroke. But my place
in that locket? I brood through the night
as much as anyone, now and then
checking the clock, enormous
with its ticking though the gears
are tiny, their little teeth catch
almost nothing. It's May,
or it's April. All afternoon
pretty much how it sounds: *all,*
then *afternoon.* The way, coming
out of surgery, I saw a room
slow and fill itself in
richly, without me.

If only those perennial opposites, the bully
and the sweet worried one
slept, kept sleeping. Not side by side,
not the lion and the lamb, just that most
ordinary blind passage, brief
and profound, as it happens
all over the planet. I mean the prince
who's happy with gardening, and the other kind
plotting someone's downfall, each
going under for the night. Which is to say, not
our usual taking turns at it, not Greenwich
or daylight savings or eight flight hours from here
equals five hours early or late but right now,
this minute, by my marvelous powers
of desperation and delusion, it's
soldier and monk, Sunni and Shiite,
republican, democrat, all Muslims and Christians
and Jews and those of us quietly
not anything to speak of, no reason or rhyme or
respectively about it, no tit for tat
but every one sleeping. And the president
curled fetal, his aides and think-tankers
all twitching in their dreams as dogs do,
on the scent or the chase, hours,
many hours to come. For that matter, the Pope is
drifting off and the greeter
from Wal-Mart, and the magician come out
of a long day's practice in a sword-crossed box
rests now, exactly like the oldest woman
asleep on her side, empty as the young docent
at Ellis Island already certain
it's robot-work, telling the country's vast sad story
of promise and trouble. And I think so many
miners home from their dark to this
gladder one, sprawled out
on their beds where exhaustion is fierce, no longer

patient. Every child in the world sleeping too,
hunger, *once there was*, but not here
in this dream, no gunflash, no flood.
Every mother minus panic. Every father
finding his daughters, his sons right where
they should be. Even
the torturers gone into that place they might
nightmare what they've done.
But not yet, not for a moment. And of those
who were done *to*, for them the rope and hood
and diamond-toothed wire, all banished
a few hours, forgotten
as dream is, in this, the real dream
to ink it out, beyond reach.
Believe me, I want to see
the despicable go down as much
as you do, and the innocent shine. But that's
sleeping too. Or so I try,
an experiment which may be stupid,
full of *less* not more, as in *pointless,* as in
hopeless, as in *less than nothing*
because—o gods of the smallest
clarity, let nothing happen
for an hour, for six hours. Rage.
Let that sleep too, its sorrow
no longer a brilliant rant, no longer anything,
a wash, a confluence of great waters
seen from a distance, the horizon a matter of
on and on where a speck out there
might well be a boat, the figure at the oars
untangling and stretching out. One eye
closed, then the other: welcome
no moon, no stars.

ACKNOWLEDGMENTS

"Still Life"; "Nice"; "O Gods of Smallest Clarity": *American Poetry Review* ("O Gods of Smallest Clarity" reprinted as a broadside, Berberis Press, 2007).

"Lunch": *Arts & Letters.*

"St. Francis in Winter": *Beloit Poetry Journal* (reprinted on *Verse Daily*).

"Relics"; "The Doctor": *The Cincinnati Review.*

"The Garden"; "A Musical Idea"; "Glenn Gould Breathing": *Crazyhorse.*

"Think of the Words"; "Simple Machines"; "Snowfall, in G Minor"; "February"; "Half Morning Song": *Field.*

"Piano, with Distance": *The Georgia Review.*

"The Park in November"; "At the Same Time": *The Gettysburg Review* ("At the Same Time" reprinted on *Poetry Daily*, "The Park in November" on *Verse Daily*).

"Learning to Read": *The Green Mountains Review.*

"New Paper"; "Minus Minus": *The Iowa Review.*

"Studying History"; "Hello": *The Kenyon Review.*

"Happiness: Three Definitions": *The Laurel Review.*

"Light on Four Sides"; "All Night": *The New England Review.*

"The Drawing Manual": *North American Review.*

"Ambition"; "Winter"; "Radio"; "In a Frame, It Matters"; "A Moment": *North Dakota Quarterly.*

"The Deer": *Ploughshares.*

"Map"; "The Body"; "After the Moon": *Poetry.*

"Omniscience"; "In the Woods: a Suite": *Prairie Schooner.*

"The Tin House": *Seneca Review.*

"Spring, in Five Parts": *TriQuarterly.*

"Seven Aubades for Summer": *Verse.*

"Elevator"; "Ladder against a House": *Virginia Quarterly Revview.*

"Telepathy"; "Yes Loves No": *The Women's Review of Books.*

"What God Knew": *The Yale Review.*

Many thanks to the editors of the above journals who first took on these poems, some in a slightly earlier form; also to the Guggenheim Foundation for the fellowship; to Purdue University for its support; to the Ragdale Foundation, the MacDowell Colony, and Eastern Frontier at Norton Island for shelter and solace. I'm deeply grateful to David and Will Dunlap, Wendy Flory, Jane Hamilton, and Susan Neville for their response to various poems, and to Brigit Kelly, Karen Brennan,

Joy Manesiotis, and Ellen Voigt for their straight talk as this book came together.   And finally: "Nice" is for June and Bill Stuckey, "Minus Minus" for Will Dunlap, "Half-Morning Song" for Susan Neville, "The Doctor" for Amanda Curnock, "The Body" for Gail Dodge, and "Learning to Read" and "Winter" for David Dunlap.

94

ABOUT THE AUTHOR

Marianne Boruch is the author of five previous collections, including *Descendant* (Wesleyan, 1989) and *Poems: New and Selected,* a finalist for the Lenore Marshall Prize from the Academy of American Poets. She has also published two books of essays on poetry, most recently *In the Blue Pharmacy.* Her poems have appeared in *The New Yorker, Kenyon Review, Iowa Review, The Yale Review, Field, The Nation* and elsewhere. Her honors include Pushcart Prizes and fellowships from the Guggenheim Foundation and the National Endowment for the Arts. She teaches in Purdue University's MFA program and in the non-residential Program for Writers at Warren Wilson College.

Library of Congress Cataloging-in-Publication Data
Boruch, Marianne, 1950–
Grace, fallen from / Marianne Boruch
    p. cm.
ISBN-13: 978–0–8195–6863–2 (cloth : alk. paper)
ISBN-10: 0–8195–6863–5 (cloth : alk. paper)
I. Title.
PS3552.075645G73 2008
811'.54—dc22   2007030905